Springwood, FDR's childhood home

HOW FRANKLIN D. ROOSEVELT GREW UP TO CHANGE AMERICA

A BOY NAMED FDR

BY KATHLEEN KRULL

ILLUSTRATED BY STEVE JOHNSON & LOU FANCHER

ALFRED A. KNOPF   New York

In memory of Eden Ross Lipson and her father, Judge Milton Lipson

—K.K.

For Joel Harris

—S.J. & L.F.

THIS IS A BORZOI BOOK PUBLISHED BY ALFRED A. KNOPF

Text copyright © 2011 by Kathleen Krull
Illustrations copyright © 2011 by Steve Johnson and Lou Fancher

All rights reserved. Published in the United States by Alfred A. Knopf, an imprint of Random House Children's Books,
a division of Random House, Inc., New York.

Knopf, Borzoi Books, and the colophon are registered trademarks of Random House, Inc.

Visit us on the Web! www.randomhouse.com/kids

Educators and librarians, for a variety of teaching tools, visit us at
www.randomhouse.com/teachers

Library of Congress Cataloging-in-Publication Data
Krull, Kathleen.
A boy named FDR : how Franklin D. Roosevelt grew up to change America / by Kathleen Krull ;
illustrated by Steve Johnson and Lou Fancher. — 1st ed.
p. cm.
ISBN 978-0-375-85716-4 (trade) — ISBN 978-0-375-95716-1 (lib. bdg.)
1. Roosevelt, Franklin D. (Franklin Delano), 1882–1945—Childhood and youth—Juvenile literature.
2. Roosevelt, Franklin D. (Franklin Delano), 1882–1945—Juvenile literature. 3. Presidents—United States—Biography—
Juvenile literature. I. Johnson, Steve, ill. II. Fancher, Lou, ill. III. Title.
E807.K78 2010
973.917092—dc22
[B]
2009022089

The illustrations in this book were created using oil and ink on gessoed paper.

MANUFACTURED IN CHINA
January 2011
10 9 8 7 6 5 4 3 2
First Edition

ONE OF HISTORY'S MYSTERIES is why President Franklin D. Roosevelt did so much for ordinary people in America. After all, he was the ultimate rich kid. He could have coasted into a sparkling future where he didn't have to work or care much about others.

When he headed into politics, most people expected it was to make the rich richer. Instead, as president during two of our most frightening times, the Great Depression and World War II, he reached out to everyone. His leadership was so extraordinary that he was able to introduce a dramatic "New Deal" for Americans, changing their relationship to their government.

At the time, some wealthy people grew so angry at him they couldn't speak his name. He was "that man in the White House."

Today, though, many historians rank FDR as one of our three most inspirational presidents, alongside George Washington and Abraham Lincoln.

So how did FDR, the boy, become FDR, our thirty-second president?

All children like to think they're the center of their universe. But a boy named FDR really was. At his birth in 1882, everyone gathered around and marveled:

"Plump, pink, and nice."

"A beautiful little fellow . . . strong and well-behaved."

"A good boy."

"A very nice child . . . always bright and happy. Not crying, worrying."

He had a fancy name—Franklin Delano Roosevelt. He slept in a fancy hand-carved cradle. He drank out of a fancy silver cup from Russia. He had long blond curls and wore dresses with fancy lace collars until he was almost six. Fancy FDR.

His parents, Sara and elderly James, had much to give to their beloved only child. Their primary home, among several, was called Springwood, in Hyde Park, New York. Perched above the Hudson River, the estate was surrounded by thick woods and a thousand-acre farm. FDR had his choice of nine bathrooms.

By his second Christmas, he would stand next to Mama, handing out toys to the children of their servants. Yes, they had many—nurses, private teachers, butlers, cooks, housekeepers, workers who took care of the horses, cattle, and land.

As for his own gifts, all he had to say was that he wanted something and it was given to him.

One of his earliest memories was crossing the Atlantic Ocean to Europe with Mama and Popsy. One night a rough storm came up. As water seeped into their cabin, Mama cuddled baby FDR in her fur coat. Then she waded in to save his favorite toy, a jumping jack, as it bobbed in the water. Anything to keep her son happy.

Safely back at home, she taught him herself, reading daily from favorite books like *Robinson Crusoe* and *The Swiss Family Robinson*. She lavished her energy on molding him into "an upstanding American." As he got older, she arranged his day around lessons, with tutors coming to the mansion to teach him every possible subject.

By six he was writing letters to Mama in French and German, signing them "FDR."

Popsy took baby FDR outdoors, jaunting about in a Russian sleigh. He learned early on how to ride horses, ice-skate, and sail a boat. Popsy taught him to hunt, the popular sport for rich gentlemen. FDR had his own pony, Debby, and a dog, a red setter named Marksman. He mastered every detail of their care.

He perfected the art of being cheerful, especially as Popsy's health declined and it became important not to worry him. Once, injured by a falling curtain rod, he insisted Popsy not be told and calmly asked for a hat so he could hide the wound.

FDR knew presidents firsthand. During a visit to the White House, President Grover Cleveland, an old family friend, spoke to him directly: "I am making a strange wish for you. It is that you may never be president of the United States." Too much stress, he implied. But did this plant the seed with FDR, then only five years old?

He was ten when Cleveland won a second term, and he never forgot that night—being awakened by a noisy parade of men singing "Yankee Doodle." Someone wrapped him in a buffalo robe and he joined the celebration. Being president was clearly cause for the best parties!

Children of his day were sometimes spanked for bad behavior, but not FDR. A hint of parental disapproval was usually punishment enough.

The ways he found to rebel were tiny. Once he climbed to the top of a tall tree and watched as darkness fell and everyone called for him. Another time he stayed up past his bedtime and, with a friend, stole the ice cream from the grown-ups' dinner party. He did get in trouble when he played a rude practical joke on a governess he disliked—but all Popsy could bring himself to do was say, "Consider yourself spanked."

At least one of FDR's teachers, Jeanne Sandoz, tried to teach him to have sympathy for those less fortunate. Her lesson may have stuck. The same year she taught him, when he was nine, he was in Germany at a hot spring believed to have healing powers. The patients were sick adults like his father. But there was one small boy in a wheelchair who would always remember FDR giving him presents and befriending him.

Both of his parents groomed him to feel responsibility for others. When Mama brought food and clothes to the poor, she took him along. "Nothing is so helpful to ourselves as doing for others and trying to sink all selfishness," she once wrote to him.

Popsy gave speeches showing he was aware of problems in America. "Help the helpless!" he urged. "Help the poor, the widow, the orphan; help the sick, the fallen man or woman, for the sake of our common humanity. Help all who are suffering."

When FDR enjoyed something, he threw himself into it. He collected just about everything, especially stamps—eventually a million of them in 150 matching albums.

He became obsessed with birds—that is, shooting, stuffing, and classifying them. For his eleventh birthday, he begged for his own shotgun and went on to collect robins, orioles, hawks—not stopping until he had every bird native to the Hudson River Valley. On visits to his grandfather, confined to a wheelchair, FDR entertained him with bird lectures.

But his biggest love was the sea. He started drawing detailed sailboats at five, and in his teens he got his very own, the *New Moon*. He sailed it every summer day at the Roosevelts' home off the Maine coast, expertly navigating dangerous waters.

He was fourteen before Mama and Popsy could bear to let him go off to Groton, an Episcopal boarding school in Massachusetts.

Older boys immediately cornered him in a hallway and ordered him to dance, poking him with hockey sticks. He danced so hard, so fearlessly, that they soon let him go.

The boys his age were as wealthy as he was, but they had been there for two years already and had established friendships. Some mocked his excellent manners around adults and the way it took him eight months to get his first "black mark" (for talking in class). It came as a shock to FDR to feel like the outsider.

The way to fit in was to be good at football and baseball. The other boys were bigger and stronger, faster and tougher, but he never gave up team sports. It wasn't in his nature to quit. He was awarded a ribbon in his senior year—as manager of the baseball team.

That same year, he won a comic role in a play and found that he adored getting laughs onstage.

The school guided FDR toward thinking of others. He greatly admired the headmaster, Reverend Endicott Peabody, who told his students to help the less fortunate. In a day when real gentlemen didn't go into politics, Peabody preached just the opposite: "If some Groton boys do not enter political life and do something for our land, it won't be because they have not been urged."

The school brought in speakers who opened the boys' eyes to the horrors of slavery as well as present-day life in New York City's slums.

FDR joined a Missionary Society that helped people, taking responsibility for making sure an elderly black widow had food and heat and got her snow shoveled. For two summers, he taught water sports at a camp for poor boys. When he was put in charge of a dorm, he was a good leader, compassionate toward the new boys—the way he wished he'd been treated.

He looked for people to inspire him and found them in Benjamin Franklin, Thomas Jefferson, and someone from his own family—his fifth cousin Theodore Roosevelt. TR was amazing, larger than life, and FDR's biggest idol. Everyone looked up to Teddy, a hero from the Spanish-American War soaring into national politics.

One day he came to speak to FDR's classmates. "You are not entitled, either in college or after, to an ounce of privilege because you have been to Groton," TR said. "Much has been given you; therefore, we have a right to expect much from you."

More and more, words mattered to FDR. TR's made a deep impression.

VOTE
FRANKLIN
ROOSEVELT
for 1904
CLASS
COMMITTEE
CHAIR

At age eighteen, a freshman at Harvard College, he told a girlfriend's family that he wanted to go into politics and thought he could go as far as president.

A mighty dream, but it seemed more real after Cousin TR did become president. Bursting with pride, FDR took note of every detail—the zesty leadership, the call for government to give people more help, the total lack of fear.

A class in "The Forms of Public Address" had him writing a speech every two weeks. But from the famous names among the faculty, FDR received mostly C's. His time went toward the *Harvard Crimson* newspaper. He rose to editor-in-chief, enjoying his control over information on campus.

It was FDR's habit to assume that everyone liked him, and he was sure he'd make it into the most exclusive social club at Harvard. Yet in a secret ceremony, the club rejected him. He never found out the reason. But it was one more thing that spurred his sympathy for those *not* in power, the outsiders and underdogs.

After this he grew more interested in how the political system worked. He campaigned hard for class office and, after a few defeats, won his first election—chairman of the 1904 class committee.

And into his life sailed Eleanor Roosevelt. She was TR's favorite niece, and being around her was a way to get closer to his hero. But she was also a world-class listener with a big heart, blue eyes, and long blond hair.

They had met earlier when, as a four-year-old, he had given his two-year-old cousin a piggyback ride. Dancing with her when she was fourteen, he noticed that she had "a very good mind."

Now he was a senior at Harvard, and she was nineteen, active in helping the poor Jewish and Italian immigrant children in the slums of New York's Lower East Side. Although she was wealthy, she was a serious young woman whose goal was to do something useful for others.

Sometimes she arranged for him to meet her at work. "I wanted him to see how people lived," she said later. "And it worked. He saw *how people lived,* and he *never* forgot."

"E IS AN ANGEL," he wrote in his diary. They talked often about his future, and he told her that "with your help" he would be someone important someday.

After he proposed, they got married on the first day President Theodore Roosevelt had free on his calendar.

FDR studied law, then became a clerk for a Wall Street company. The only part of the job he really enjoyed was mixing with people from all kinds of backgrounds.

One afternoon at the office, he casually mentioned becoming president. But would he ever have a chance to get started?

Finally, in 1910, a spot opened up in the New York State Senate, and he was invited to run. No one (except Mama and Eleanor) thought he had a chance.

Few were more persistent than FDR. He crisscrossed Dutchess County for weeks, giving up to twenty speeches a day.

People liked him. Enough voted for him that he won, surprising nearly everyone. At age twenty-eight, he was a New York state senator, and everything about the job just tickled him. With his trademark energy and jaunty grin, he would vault over a row of chairs to get to the front of a room where he was to speak.

FDR was obsessed with following the path of his hero TR as closely as he could—New York State politics (including becoming governor of New York), assistant secretary of the navy, and eventually president.

But for him the path was not straight.

At age thirty-nine, he was stricken with the most feared disease in America—polio, a crippling infection that was then incurable. Unlike many victims, he survived—but he simply could *not* move his legs.

Imagine this most active of men, lying helpless on his back. Weeks turned into months, and no matter what he or his doctors did, his legs remained paralyzed. In pain and with moments of despair, he spent the next few years trying to walk again.

Displaying the persistence he had shown all his life, he never gave up.

With much time to think, he was overwhelmed by sympathy for other polio sufferers. One way he filled his time was by establishing a first-class treatment center for them in Warm Springs, Georgia. Besides raising the money for it, he spent time caring for the patients, doing whatever he could to lift their spirits.

For hours every day, he exercised his chest and shoulder muscles as hard as an athlete training for the Olympics. He would always appear powerful from the waist up. But for the rest of his life, he could not stand without someone helping him.

Mama wanted him to retire and live the life of a rich gentleman. But Eleanor felt exactly the opposite. His legs had weakened and shrunk, but just the opposite had happened to his mind. The terrible experience had expanded his horizons, with the potential to transform him into a special kind of leader.

It was Eleanor who urged him to get back into politics. Three years after being stricken with polio, he agreed to give a speech in public. That night, he inched his way to the stage, walking with obvious pain on his crutches. Yet he wore his trademark grin.

The crowd in front of him roared its approval of his return.

And he got back on TR's path, aiming for the White House. . . .

FRANKLIN D. ROOSEVELT, President from 1933–1945

FDR had to draw upon all the resources life had given him when it became his job to lead the country through two of its worst times. Following the crash of the stock market, the Great Depression left millions of people homeless. FDR's response, immediately after his inauguration, was to offer a series of creative programs called the New Deal. He got Congress to fund brand-new projects—giving loans to those losing their homes, establishing Social Security, a "safety net" that provided unemployment and disability insurance and pensions for the elderly. He also got Congress to raise taxes on large companies and on people with large incomes.

In his speeches and his thirty national radio broadcasts, or "fireside chats," his words radiated warmth to millions of ordinary, suffering Americans. By 1940 he was getting four thousand letters a day from them. Very few realized that he had lost the use of his legs and was masterminding the New Deal from his wheelchair.

Then came the catastrophic World War II. FDR took the lead in establishing an alliance among all countries fighting Adolf Hitler and the Axis powers, winning a solid victory that led to America's becoming the most prosperous country in the world.

Full of zest, always bubbly, FDR got impossible things done and inspired others to do the same—a figure so indispensable to the average American that he was elected president four times, serving longer than any other president.

FDR'S LIFE AND FAMOUS WORDS

January 30, 1882 Franklin Delano Roosevelt was born at Springwood,
  in Hyde Park, New York
1900 Graduated from Groton School
1904 Graduated from Harvard College
1905 Entered Columbia Law School; married Eleanor Roosevelt
1906 Anna Eleanor, the first of their six children, was born
1907 Started as a clerk for a prominent Wall Street law firm
1910 Elected to the New York State Senate
1913 Appointed assistant secretary of the navy
1920 Nominated for vice president, but his team lost the election to Warren G. Harding
1921 Stricken with polio
1924 Returned to public life and managed the presidential campaign of Alfred E. Smith
1928 Elected governor of New York

Modern society, acting through its government, owes the definite obligation to prevent the starvation or the dire want of any of its fellow men and women who try to maintain themselves but cannot. (Speech as governor, 1931)

1929 The American stock market crashed
1932 Elected as thirty-second president

I pledge you, I pledge myself, to a new deal for the American people. (Speech accepting the nomination for president, 1932)

This great nation will endure as it has endured, will revive and will prosper. So, first of all, let me assert my firm belief that the only thing we have to fear is fear itself—nameless, unreasoning, unjustified terror, which paralyzes needed efforts to convert retreat into advance. In every dark hour of our national life, a leadership of frankness and vigor has met with that understanding and support of the people themselves, which is essential to victory. (First Inaugural Address, 1933)

1936 Reelected for second term as president

To some generations much is given. Of other generations much is expected. This generation of Americans has a rendezvous with destiny. (Speech to the Democratic National Convention, Philadelphia, Pennsylvania, 1936)

I see one-third of a nation ill-housed, ill-clad, ill-nourished. . . . The test of our progress is not whether we add more to the abundance of those who have much; it is whether we provide enough for those who have too little. (Second Inaugural Address, 1937)

1940 Reelected for third term as president

Yesterday, December 7, 1941—a date which will live in infamy . . .
(Message to Congress following declaration of war after the Japanese attack on Pearl Harbor, 1941)

We look forward to a world founded upon four essential human freedoms. The first is freedom of speech and expression. . . . The second is freedom of every person to worship God in his own way. . . . The third is freedom from want. . . . The fourth is freedom from fear. (Message to Congress, 1941)

Never before have we had so little time in which to do so much. (Fireside chat, 1942)

Books cannot be killed by fire. People die, but books never die. No man and no force can abolish memory. (Message to the American Booksellers Association, 1942)

Future generations will know that here, in the middle of the twentieth century, there came a time when men of good will found a way to unite, and produce, and fight to destroy the forces of ignorance, and intolerance, and slavery, and war. (Speech, 1943)

1944 Reelected for fourth term as president

The trend of civilization itself is forever upward. (Fourth Inaugural Address, 1945)

April 12, 1945 Died of a stroke at age 63 in Warm Springs, Georgia

August 15, 1945 Japan surrendered, ending World War II

SOURCES

Alter, Jonathan. *The Defining Moment: FDR's Hundred Days and the Triumph of Hope.* New York: Simon & Schuster, 2006.

Brands, H. W. *Traitor to His Class: The Privileged Life and Radical Presidency of Franklin Delano Roosevelt.* New York: Doubleday, 2008.

Franklin and Eleanor Roosevelt Institute, www.feri.org

Franklin D. Roosevelt Presidential Library and Museum, www.fdrlibrary.marist.edu

*Freedman, Russell. *Franklin Delano Roosevelt.* New York: Clarion, 1990.

Groton School, www.groton.org/home/home.asp

Harvard University, www.harvard.edu

*Panchyk, Richard. *Franklin Delano Roosevelt for Kids: His Life and Times with 21 Activities.* Chicago: Chicago Review Press, 2007.

Parker, Stamford. *The Words That Reshaped America: FDR.* New York: Quill, 2000.

Smith, Jean Edward. *FDR.* New York: Random House, 2007.

*St. George, Judith. *Make Your Mark, Franklin Roosevelt.* New York: Philomel, 2007.

Ward, Geoffrey C. *Before the Trumpet: Young Franklin Roosevelt, 1882–1905.* New York: HarperCollins, 1985.

*especially for young readers